Drew's New Seeds

By Carmel Reilly

Drew liked to grow blooms.

He grew red ones and
yellow ones.

Drew put dirt in pots
and planted a few seeds.

He wet them so the seeds
would grow.

If the wind blew too hard,
Drew put his pots inside.

Drew liked to try new kinds of seeds.

One day, the plant shop lady gave him a blank pack.

"What is it?" Drew said.

"Wait and see," said the lady.
"It's **not** a bloom!"

Drew planted the new seeds
in a big pot.

He checked the pot
each day.

The seeds grew and grew
into buds.

Each bud turned into
a red berry.

Mum picked a berry
to chew on.

"This would be great
in a stew," said Mum.

"Or jam," said Drew.

"They are not ripe just yet," said Mum.

n a few days, Drew went
out to pick the berry plant.

But some birds were eating
every berry!

Drew scared them off
with a rake.

When the birds flew away,
the plant had no red left!

I see a few they did not eat,"
said Mum.

"We can make **one** jar of jam!"
said Drew, with a grin.

CHECKING FOR MEANING

1. What did Drew like to do? *(Literal)*

2. Who gave Drew the blank pack of seeds? *(Literal)*

3. Why do you think the birds liked eating the berries? *(Inferential)*

EXTENDING VOCABULARY

blooms	What are *blooms*? What is another word that has a similar meaning? E.g. flowers.
blew	What does *blew* mean? Explain that *blew* is the past tense of the verb *blow*. In a similar way, *grew* is the past-tense form of the verb *grow*.
stew	What is a *stew*? What foods go into making a stew? Have you ever eaten a stew? How did it taste? E.g. delicious, tasty, healthy.

MOVING BEYOND THE TEXT

1. Explain what you need to do to grow plants from seeds.

2. What plants have you grown at home or at school? How and where did you grow them?

3. Why do people like growing plants? What do they do with them when they are grown?

4. What could Drew have done to stop the birds getting the berries?

SPEED SOUNDS

oo	ue	ew	ui	u_e

ou	u	oe	o

PRACTICE WORDS

Drew

to

blooms

grew

few

blew

too

new

chew

stew

flew

bloom